OWN

YOUR

TRUE

WORTH

Other Books by Victoria Reynolds

Transcending Fear

Free Your Spirit

Rise Up

Recreating Earth

Little Marigold

Fearless and Free

OWN
YOUR
TRUE
WORTH
Vital Keys to Living
Your Full Value

VICTORIA REYNOLDS

Own Your True Worth: Vital Keys to Living Your Full Value

Updated September 2025

Freestyle Press
A Division of Luminary Media Group

ISBN: 978-1-954250-03-1 (sb)
ISBN: 978-1-954250-04-8 (ebk)

Freestyle Press

"... there is a common thread that runs through all of our pain and all of our suffering, and that is unworthiness. Not feeling worthy enough to own the life you were created for. Even people who believe they deserve to be happy and have nice things often don't feel worthy once they have them."

- **Oprah Winfrey**

TABLE OF CONTENTS

INTRODUCTION 1

    The Mastery of Worth 1

THE 1ST KEY 17

    Discover Belief vs. Truth 17

THE 2ND KEY...35

    Understand Your Narrative 35

THE 3RD KEY...55

    Realize the Power of Story.................................. 55

THE 4TH KEY...73

    Accept Your Whole Self 73

THE 5TH KEY...89

    Reclaim Your Power... 89

THE 6TH KEY... 107

    Practice Self-Centeredness 107

THE 7TH KEY.. 125

    Internalize Your True Worth 125

CONCLUSION... 141

    You Were Always Worthy 141

ABOUT THE AUTHOR.. 145

INTRODUCTION
The Mastery of Worth

I never set out to become a teacher of worthiness and personal value. It wasn't until I began to uncover how deeply my own unconscious beliefs of unworthiness were playing out, limiting my ability to step into the roles I felt calling me, that I understood the magnitude of their influence.

True success — the kind I felt aligned

with my soul's greater purpose — was always in sight, yet just beyond reach. I could feel the vision pulling me. I could clearly see it just above the horizon. But something kept tugging at me from below, pulling me back into an invisible cycle I couldn't seem to escape. Even with years of self-help books and working through my shadows, there was still something I couldn't shake.

That something was the unconscious plague of unworthiness.

Several years ago, I began tracing the roots of this seemingly unshakable feeling that what I saw as real success, matching my life's purpose, would never become my reality, even when the greater purpose for my life was shown so clearly to me. I discovered what I now recognize as one of the most destructive patterns woven through the human condition, preventing the joy that is every person's birthright.

It is a quiet, persistent, and pervasive epidemic that keeps countless people from reaching their divine potential — and worse, convinces many not to even try.

Like so many others, I had to learn the hard way how to move forward — by confronting the stories that confined me.

Stories like:

- Not good enough — I was born to the wrong family, in the wrong place, with the wrong belief system.

- Not smart enough — I wasn't educated in the right ways or didn't make the "right" choices.

- Not perfect enough — If I weren't more polished, better read, more prepared, then men, business partners, potential clients, or even God wouldn't take me seriously.

- Not pretty enough — And because

beauty seemed to define success, I couldn't see my own power.

- Not masculine enough — I believed I had to dress and act like a man to succeed in a man's world.

- Not successful enough — My previous ventures had never grown to the level of success that made me proud to be their founder. This lack of success made me feel unworthy of future success.

- Too young, too old. Too inexperienced, then too experienced.

- The thread beneath them all? I wasn't

worthy of the life I desired.

Not worthy of love. Not worthy of peace, freedom, joy, or success. And certainly not worthy of leadership.

These weren't thoughts I sat and ruminated over. Sometimes they were fleeting moments that flashed by and didn't stay long enough to ponder. They didn't stick in my conscious mind.

Instead, they were beliefs held as truths written into my nervous system — intergenerational and family scripts passed down through culture, religion, trauma, and tradition. I didn't choose them, but I lived them as if I had.

They were **hand-me-down** beliefs.

And that's where this journey begins.

Where Worthlessness Begins

Unworthiness begins and lodges itself in our subconscious, long before adulthood. It begins with the moment we internalize a message — spoken or silent — that tells us our value is conditional. That we are worth less until we prove otherwise. That we must become, achieve, or sacrifice something to finally be "enough."

These beliefs and stories rarely originate with us. They are passed forward through generations and societal conditioning, from parent to child, from teacher to student, from culture to mind — encoded in systems, reinforced through shame, and embedded in silence.

They live in the body. They influence who we love, how we speak, what we charge, what we tolerate, and how we lead. Until we question them, they operate as truth.

The Evolution of This Work

Own Your True Worth began years ago as a simple guide to help people name their internal struggles and reclaim their value. Like my earlier books — Transcending Fear and Free Your Spirit — it came from personal excavation and a desire to help others find their way back to themselves.

As I've grown, so has the message. Today, I no longer write as a coach or healer. I lead as a media executive, public voice, and cultural architect. And with that shift has come an even more profound realization: Owning your worth is not just a personal journey. It is a leadership imperative.

You cannot fully lead others — not your children, your clients, your team, or your vision — if you are still questioning your own value.

Unworthiness leaks. It shows up in how we discount ourselves, defer to others, apologize for existing, or silence our truth to avoid discomfort. It grips the throat. It hides behind "niceness." It wears the mask of humility. And it robs the world of our brilliance.

This Book Is a Map Back to Self

The seven keys in this book are not just steps to healing — they are doorways to liberation. Each one invites you to:

- Remember your inherent value

- Realign your internal compass

- Reclaim your voice, your vision, and your value

- And restore the limitless potential you were always meant to express

These keys will help you:

- Recognize where unworthiness began — in both your lineage and life

- Release inherited beliefs that no longer serve

- Rewrite your inner narrative

- Return to your sovereignty and clarity

- And fully own the value of being you

Whether you are healing from old childhood wounds, emerging from spiritual confusion, navigating leadership in uncertain times, or done playing small — this book will help you rise.

You don't need another strategy. You need a new and improved story. One that begins and ends with your unshakable value.

You Are the Proof

You were never broken. You don't need to be fixed, rescued, or validated. What you need — what the world needs — is your presence. Whole. Integrated. Embodied

That begins with owning your worth. Not just affirming it. Not waiting for you to feel ready. But living it. Leading with it. Letting it speak through everything you do.

This is your moment to remember: You are the author of your worth. And your story is just getting started.

Journaling Your Progress

At the end of each chapter, I provide journal pages for reflection questions and practices to recognize past limiting beliefs, build your personal value and mark your progress.

KEY #1
DISCOVER

THE 1ST KEY
Discover Belief vs. Truth

Discovering the difference between belief and truth is finding your authentic self.

Owning your true worth means remembering the value of who you were at the moment of your birth — and reclaiming who you were always meant to be.

This is your authentic self: not the roles you were assigned, not the expectations placed upon you, and not the version of you shaped by survival. Your true self may be radically different than the persona you've lived through most of your life.

To own your worth is to take full and complete ownership of your inherent value. It means internalizing—through thought, feeling, action, and knowing—that you are intrinsically worthy of everything your heart desires. Your value is not conditional, performative, or dependent on anyone else's opinion. It is the truth of who you are.

Self-worth is the perception of value we hold about ourselves, shaped by our early experiences and how others responded to our basic human needs. From infancy, we unconsciously track our worth through the cues we receive — through touch, voice, eye contact, presence, and attention.

A newborn who is not held will eventually fail to thrive. Human beings are wired for connection, not because our egos crave validation, but because love is essential to our well-being. As social beings, our sense of belonging and value is biologically encoded into our survival systems.

When we are neglected, criticized, or punished in childhood — especially by those we rely on most — our nervous systems store the message: "I must not be enough." These early messages form the foundation of our core beliefs, and over time, we come to see ourselves through the lens of those beliefs.

As children, what we crave most is to be loved, seen, accepted, and safe. That bond typically begins with our primary caregiver — usually our mother — and creates a foundation for whether or not we feel worthy of love. When that connection is disrupted, replaced with harm, criticism, emotional neglect, or material substitution, the child begins to form stories about their worth.

Even the most well-intentioned parents may unconsciously pass down beliefs rooted in fear or lack. These become what I call "hand-me-down beliefs." Beliefs such as:

- I am bad

- I am too much, too loud, too curious, too independent, too energetic, too pensive. I ask too many questions.

- I am not enough, I'm not good enough, I'm not smart enough, I don't work hard enough, I'm not silent enough, I'm not righteous enough, I'm not tough enough.

• I must earn love, I have to prove myself to be accepted by the adults around me and by God

• I must not speak up. It's safer to keep my thoughts and feelings to myself.

Children act out, not because they are bad or broken, but because they are trying to get the attention they need to survive. In the mind of a child, attention equals value. Negative attention, even punishment, can reinforce an unconscious belief: "This pain is what I deserve." That belief becomes part of their inner operating system.

As we grow, we internalize more subtle forms of messaging—from school, religion, media, peers, and culture. Beliefs compound. What starts as a single moment of shame becomes a lifetime pattern of self-rejection.

Eventually, unworthiness becomes so familiar that we no longer question it. It becomes the default for how we move through life, completely unaware that the narrative running our lives is a culmination of false beliefs.

Many adults find themselves triggered

by life situations—rejection, abandonment, failure—and feel an internal collapse that seems out of proportion to the moment. That is the younger self trying to protect itself from more pain. What appears to be anger or defensiveness is often a symptom of long-held beliefs surfacing for healing.

What appears as "I'm not meant for happiness, prosperity or success" is unworthiness, justifying itself. It is fear showing itself for resolution. It is old beliefs asking us if we are willing to stand in the face of unworthiness and transform it.

Here's the good news:

What was learned can be unlearned.

What was inherited can be released.

What was hidden can be reclaimed.

What is true can become embodied.

When you begin to see the patterns for what they are—beliefs, not truth—you open the door to change. When you witness your inner responses with compassion rather than judgment, you become the leader of your own healing. And when you consciously choose new beliefs, you begin to shift how you show up in the world.

To discover your authentic self is to strip away the layers of false programming, pain, and performance. It's not about fixing who you are—it's about remembering who you've always been beneath the stories.

You don't have to prove your worth. You only have to own it.

Reflection Questions:

• What moments from childhood shaped your beliefs about being "not enough"?

• Whose voices still echo in your mind, and do they reflect the truth of who you are?

• Where in your life are you still seeking permission to be worthy?

_____

_____

_____

_____

_____

_____

Practice - Free Flow Writing:

Now, free-write a description of yourself that has nothing to do with your performance, roles, expectations, or achievements. Let the words speak from the soul.

Write in the voice of your highest truth — as if you were remembering yourself, the true essence of your divine self, not reinventing who you wish you had been.

Who you were, and what you once believed, is just a stepping stone on the map to becoming who you were always meant to be.

KEY #2
UNDERSTAND

THE 2ND KEY
Understand Your Narrative

Understanding the power of your inner story and narrative beings to transform how you view everything in life. We don't experience life as it is. We experience life through the perspective lens of the stories we tell ourselves.

These inner narratives — shaped by our past, our parents, our culture, and our conditioning — form the architecture of how we see the world and our place in it. They are often invisible, but their impact is profound. They dictate how we interpret events, what we believe we're capable of, and whether we feel worthy of receiving what we desire.

When your narrative is rooted in unworthiness, it tells you things like:

- "I always mess things up."

- "I've failed at everything I've ever tried."

- "No one really sees or values me."

- "I'm too late, too old, too damaged."

- "Success is for other people, not for

me."

These are not harmless thoughts. They are codes of self-identity — quiet scripts that shape your choices, reactions, relationships, and ability to lead. They keep you trapped in an imaginary world of negative projection. A script and a screen that are just a reflection of who you think you are, based on what you believe others believe about you.

The Narrative Within

Our inner narrative is more than just a mindset. It is the emotional and energetic programming we internalized in our earliest years, shaped by:

- What we were told

- What we weren't told

- How we were treated

- What we told ourselves about the past

- What we had to suppress in order to survive

Many of us grew up hearing that we were too much or not enough, and sometimes both. We were taught to stay small to be safe, silent to be accepted, obedient to be loved. Those survival strategies became internal stories.

Over time, those stories became our identity. But here's the truth: your current story is not your final story. And it was never your only story. It was all just a backstory that carved a narrative for who you are today, and helped to cultivate who you choose to become.

You can choose to cling to your backstory as your identity, or you can see it as an inspiring story of strength, resilience, overcoming, and empowerment in the face of adversity and the stories of your past. Almost everyone has a painful backstory. It's what you do with the story that makes all the difference.

You are not the sum of your conditioning. You are the author of your consciousness.

The Cost of a Worth-less Story

When we carry a core belief that we are not enough, everything we do is colored by that frequency. We:

- Undervalue our contributions

- Undercharge for our services

- Over-give in relationships

- Stay silent when we should speak

- Say yes when our body says no

- Apologize for taking up space

Why do we hold onto these patterns? Because they are familiar. Because they once protected us. Because our nervous systems are wired for safety, and change — even positive change — can feel unsafe when we're not used to it.

But the truth is this: there are few things more dangerous than living a life built on a lie about who you are.

Naming the Story Isn't Enough

Awareness is important. But it's only the open doorway, and not the destination.

To truly rewrite the narrative, we have to go deeper than surface affirmations or attempted mindset hacks. We must move from intellectual understanding to embodied truth.

That means:

- Feeling where the old story lives in the body

- Giving voice to the parts of ourselves that were silenced

- Holding compassion for the younger self who did the best she or he could

- Forgiving ourselves for not knowing what we could not have possibly known

- Choosing — again and again — to speak and act from the truth of our wholeness

You can't think your way into a new identity. You must live your way into it.

Overwrite the Narrative

Become the author of your inner world. When you begin to understand that your story is not fixed — that it's something you can co-create — you take back your power.

Rewriting your story doesn't mean pretending everything is fine. It means telling a more whole, honest story. A story that includes the pain and the power. A story that honors where you've been and where you're going.

It's not about toxic positivity. It's about your sacred authorship. Language is frequency. Words are creation. The words you speak to yourself shape your world.

Reflection Questions:

• What stories have you told yourself about who you are, what you deserve, and what's possible?

• Where did those stories originate?

• Who would you be without that story?

_____

_____

_____

_____

_____

_____

_____

Practice: Rewrite the Story

Divide the journal page in half. On the left side, write the version of your life you've unconsciously lived until now — the one shaped by fear, lack, rejection, or shame. Don't hold back. Let the old story come to the surface.

On the right side, write the story that's waiting to be told — the one where you are the author of your worth, not the victim of your past. Let your higher self take the pen.

Then speak that new story aloud. Not just once — but until it lives in your cells.

You are the narrator now. And your story

has just begun.

_____

_____

_____

_____

_____

_____

_____

_____

_____

_____

KEY #3
REALIZE

THE 3RD KEY
Realize the Power of Story

You are not your stories. You are not your trauma. You are not your role, your reputation, your accomplishments or your resume. You are not your past, your projections, or even your personality.

You are a soul — whole, wise, and sovereign — who temporarily forgot who you were. You are spirit, divine energy experiencing itself in human form, adopting a personality to experience life through. This is the moment you begin to remember.

Soul vs. Survival Identity

From the moment you were born, you were fully intact. You were whole, born with everything you need to fulfill a life of purpose, as designed by your soul. But very quickly, your environment began shaping your experience of self. You learned what was safe to express, what earned love, and what parts of you needed to be hidden to belong.

Your survival identity formed to protect you. It helped you adapt. It became self-preservation. It helped you stay attached and connected even when the connection came at the cost of your truth.

But adaptation is not the same as authenticity. And survival is not the same as sovereignty.

The stories you internalized — the ones that told you who you needed to be, in order for others to accept you — were never the full truth. They were roles, not your reality. Protective layers, not your essence. It is time now to lay down those roles.

The Illusion of the Mask

The wounded self wears many masks:

- The achiever

- The perfectionist

- The peacekeeper

- The over-giver

- The invisible one

- The quiet one

- The-over-talker

- The strong one who never asks for

  help

Each of these personas was built to cope with a world that didn't see your wholeness. They were brilliant adaptations. They kept you safe. But they are not who you are.

The danger of these roles is that, over time, we forget they were roles at all. We believe the performance. We identify with the mask. And in doing so, we limit the expression of our true self — the self that is not bound by shame, duty, fear, or desperation to be acknowledged.

The truth is this: you are not broken – you never work. You are brilliant. You were meant to shine. And you are remembering.

This realization is not just a spiritual epiphany — it's a lived reclamation.

Awakening Without Bypassing

Realizing who you are doesn't mean pretending your pain never happened. It means seeing and understanding that the pain shaped your path, but it does not define your potential.

This is not about escaping your humanity. It's about embodying your divinity through your humanity.

There is a version of spirituality that

bypasses recognition and working through pain in favor of positive thinking and "it's all good." This is not that. This path honors the grief, the fear, the rage — and integrates it into a wholeness that holds space for all of you.

You are not returning to who you used to be. You are becoming who you were always meant to be, before life pulled you into the false illusions of belief. You are remembering who you really are. Whole, complete, and in the perfect process of growth.

Realization as a Turning Point

To realize is to awaken. To see clearly what was hidden. To remember what was once forgotten. This is a moment of deep reconnection.

You are not the story. You are the storyteller. You are not the mask. You are the one beneath it. You are not the wound. You are the wisdom it forged. You no longer have to be the person who survived. You are the one who is here to live.

Deserving and Receiving

One of the most powerful realizations you can make is this: we don't get what we want — we get what we believe we deserve.

What you project outward through your energy, thoughts, words, and actions tells the universe what to serve back to you. The frequency of your self-perception, your beliefs in deservedness, sets the tone for what life delivers.

Successful people often carry an unshakable knowing that they deserve success. Even if they once doubted themselves, that doubt was replaced with a deeper belief: " I am worthy of having what I desire."

Deserving is not about entitlement. It's about energetic permission. If you don't believe you deserve love, wealth, health, joy, or recognition, you will unconsciously block it, deflect it, or self-sabotage the moment it tries to enter.

When you realize that worth is not something you earn — but something you own — you begin to allow life to serve you accordingly. This is not about ego. It's about alignment.

You were born worthy of everything

you desire. You couldn't even imagine it if the possibilities and potential didn't already exist.

You've always been deserving. Now it's time to live like it.

Reflection Questions:

- What masks or roles have you worn to be accepted, validated, or safe?

- What parts of yourself have you hidden, suppressed, or edited to fit into someone else's story?

- What do you sense is the truth of your soul identity?

- Where have you been seeing yourself as undeserving or judging others for getting what you don't think they deserve? (Projections of judgment are reflections of how we judge ourselves.)

Practice: Soul Recognition

Stand in front of a mirror. Look into your own eyes. Not at your hair, or your flaws, or your surface. Look into the depths.

Say aloud: "I see you. I remember you. You are not your pain. You are not your past. You are the one who is rising." Allow yourself to feel into those words, allow yourself to grieve, and breathe into the truth you may have never given yourself.

Then, write in your journal:

- What came up as I spoke to myself in the mirror?

- What does my soul want me to know today?

Let your soul write the answers. Don't filter. Don't fix. Let it flow. This free-form writing will bring up what is ready to be remedied, and love you through the process.

This is your moment of realization. The stories are not you. But the truth of who you are is finally ready to be seen.

KEY #4
ACCEPT

THE 4TH KEY
Accept Your Whole Self

Now that you know where your perceptions of self-worth came from, let's get to work on restoring your true value.

Making peace with your past and present opens the door to a whole new future—one built on self-acceptance, rather than self-judgment and self-rejection. It means coming to terms with your own greatness, your true brilliance, and recognizing the magnificence that has always lived within you.

Embracing the Past

For many people, their past, with its experiences and perceptions, plays an overwhelming role in shaping how they perceive themselves. This self-perception may be radically different from how others perceive us.

Childhood wounds, painful memories, past failures, and even family history or cultural lineage shape a self-image rooted in limitation.

But simply attempting to "put the past behind you" doesn't guarantee healing. True freedom comes from processing the past — not avoiding it. The only way to get past the past, is to work your way through it.

When you're ready to move forward in life, you're also being invited to examine everything that shaped your current perception of self. That includes revisiting personal, family, and cultural stories, painful memories, hurtful experiences, and emotions that were once buried or only acknowledged through a victim's perspective.

Revisiting the stories and bringing them up for review isn't to relive the pain, but to release the power the pain once had over you.

The past becomes invaluable when you accept it as the curriculum of your personal evolution. Every moment of your story holds meaning. Every challenge was a teacher. And only you get to decide when the lesson is complete.

The lesson is complete when you can look back and say, "Thank you for what you taught me," even if it was painful at the time.

Accepting Others

Part of reclaiming your worth is releasing the grip of what others did — or didn't do. It's not about condoning harmful behavior. It's about releasing the fantasy that it should have been different. You can't change the past. But you can change your relationship with it.

Acceptance means seeing others as human beings doing the best they could with what they knew. Even those who caused harm were, in their own way, trying to survive. That doesn't excuse their behavior. It simply means you're no longer waiting for them to change in order for you to heal.

It means no longer willing to hold yourself captive under the weight of other people's choices. The choices and actions of others do not define you. They were who they were, and they are who they are. You get to choose who you are and you will be moving forward.

This is the moment you give yourself permission to be free.

Radical Self-Acceptance

Choosing radical self-acceptance can create a new baseline for your life. Most importantly, acceptance means turning inward — with self- compassion. True self-worth is born not from fixing who you are, but from loving who you are. It means saying:

"I accept the whole of me."

"I accept what I've done and what I didn't do."

"I accept my strength and I accept my sensitivity."

"I accept my past not as punishment, but as preparation."

You don't need to be perfect to be powerful.

You don't need to be finished to be worthy.

You simply need to accept that you are in process — and that process is sacred.

Self-acceptance leads to loving self-appreciation. And self-appreciation leads to true, embodied value.

Reflection Questions:

- What parts of your past story are still influencing how you see yourself today?

- What people or experiences have you been resisting, hoping they'd be different?

- What would it feel like to accept yourself without condition?

_____

_____

_____

_____

_____

_____

_____

Practice: Letter to the Past

Write a letter to a version of yourself you have judged, abandoned, or tried to forget. It could be your teenage self, your child self, or a version of you that made mistakes.

Tell that version:

- What you now see

- What you forgive

- What you appreciate

Let it be raw. Let it be real. Let this be your

bridge to peace. When you are done, say aloud:

"I accept you. I love you. We are whole now."

This is how self-worth returns — through the frequency of full, radical acceptance.

_____

_____

_____

_____

_____

_____

_____

_____

KEY #5
RECLAIM

THE 5TH KEY
Reclaim Your Power

It's time to reclaim your true power and absolute presence. You've remembered your worth. You've rewritten the story. You've accepted the whole of who you are. Now comes the reclamation.

To reclaim is to retrieve what was lost, silenced, stolen, or given away. It's gathering back the parts of yourself you tucked away for safety, or disowned because of self-judgment. The voice you quieted to avoid ridicule The power you outsourced to parents, partners, pastors, bosses, or systems. The visibility you denied yourself because it felt dangerous to shine.

Reclaiming is not about becoming something new — it's about returning to the truth of who you've always been. It's being true to yourself. Its ownership, and in ownership, there is power.

You Were Born Powerful

As children, we were naturally radiant —
alive with curiosity, creativity, joy, and self-
trust. We sang, loud and bold, without
shame. We spoke without rehearsing. We
loved freely and believed in the beauty of
our own dreams. Then life taught us to dim.

We gave away pieces of ourselves for
safety, love, approval, and survival. We
internalized stories that taught us to stay
small, stay silent, stay safe.

But the truth is: your voice is your
power. Your presence is your power. Your
joy is your power. It's time to reclaim what
never should have been hidden.

Gratitude as a Gateway

Owning your true worth and your true value ignites what it means to really live. It restores your aliveness.

Those who are able to see all of who they are — including their past — through new eyes, begin to feel fully alive again. They access a vibrancy they haven't felt since childhood, before misperceptions and fear-based beliefs got in the way.

And the key to reclaiming that vibrancy? Gratitude. Gratitude changes your perception — and your perception creates your reality.

This is internal work. As before, this isn't about spiritual bypass or surface-level "positivity." This is about using gratitude as a powerful force for transformation.

It means seeing even the painful parts of your story through a loving lens. It allows you to grieve through your life in review. It will enable you to feel the pain, without resentment, as you release attachments to how life "should" have been.

It means asking:

- What did this experience teach me?

- What value can I extract from what I once resented?

Gratitude is not about being thankful for the pain. It's about being grateful through the pain — and for the wisdom it left behind. This hard-earned and gained wisdom chisels you into the masterpiece you are becoming.

Appreciation Expands Value

Gratitude says, "Thank you." Appreciation says, "You are valuable."

Appreciation isn't the same as gratitude. Where gratitude is the acknowledgment of something received, appreciation is an energetic elevation — it raises the perceived value of what is being focused on. Just as depreciation lowers the value of an asset, appreciation raises it.

When you begin to appreciate yourself, you raise your own perceived worth — both internally and externally. That shift radiates outward. It affects how you price your services, how you speak about your work and your desired clients, how you show up in relationships, and how you receive abundance.

Appreciation shifts your frequency. It

opens your field to receive more. When you appreciate yourself — your gifts, your experiences, your journey — the world begins to reflect that higher value back to you.

You become a magnet for your own radiance.

You raise your voice.

You raise your prices.

You raise your boundaries.

You raise your vibration.

And you begin to live from a place of knowing, not needing.

Appreciation becomes a frequency

that radiates from your very being. It draws in perfectly aligned opportunities, people, and experiences — because you are finally a match for the value you carry.

The Power of Love

Seeing life through the eyes of love changes everything.

Love expands. fear contracts

Gratitude fills. Complaining drains.

Appreciation enriches. Judgment diminishes

When you reclaim the power of love-based perception, you become the sovereign creator of your reality — not the passive

recipient of it.

Reflection Questions:

- What parts of yourself have you given away in exchange for approval or safety?

- What gifts have you overlooked because you didn't think they had value?

- What would change in your reality if you fully appreciated your own presence in the world?

_____

_____

_____

Practice: Reclamation Inventory

It's time to reclaim your power. In your journal, create sections:

- **What** I Gave Away — Voice, visibility, trust, softness, dreams, etc.

- **Why** I Gave It Away — Fear, survival, family dynamics, societal pressure

- **How** I Reclaim It Now — Speaking up, setting boundaries, making art, raising prices, sharing my story, etc.

Then close your eyes and speak aloud:

"I call all of my power back to me — from

people, stories, systems, and seasons. I lovingly restore all disowned aspects back into my wholeness. I reclaim what is mine. I own my worth. I live from truth. And I welcome the life that's been waiting for me."

This is your time to rise in the fullness of who you are.

KEY #6
PRACTICE

THE 6TH KEY
Practice Self-Centeredness

Everything in your life reflects the relationship you have with yourself.

Owning your true worth begins by creating a loving, intentional relationship with every part of who you are. It means no longer judging any aspect of yourself, even the parts you've hidden or tried to pretend don't exist, because you saw them as unworthy, unlovable, or undeserving. It means learning to love ALL of you, even the perceived broken pieces and less-than-loving choices of the past.

This means learning how to care for yourself, speak lovingly to yourself, and value yourself—consistently. This also means learning the difference between selfishness and self-centeredness.

Selfishness is taking at the expense of others. Self-centeredness is being centered, and rooted within yourself—so fully resourced that what you give to others flows from overflow, not depletion.

The more you tend to your inner world, the more your outer world reflects that care. People who are self-centered in the true sense are deeply grounded. Their generosity is not a performance — it's an extension of wholeness.

This is the practice: becoming so centered in your own worth that everything you give is an act of love, not an obligation, and not from ego in need of validating. Your work becomes service, not sacrifice. Your relationships become mutual, not codependent.

Everything you touch is an extension

of how you love yourself. Self-love is love sourced from within. Self-love includes:

- Self-forgiveness

- Self-compassion

- Self-respect

- Self-honor

- Self-trust

- Self-kindness

- Self-acceptance

- Self-appreciation

- Self-care

- Self-awareness

- Self-realization

The more you embody these qualities, the

more magnetic you become. Your life begins to mirror back the worth you hold internally.

Below are two foundational practices to help reestablish that worth and rebuild trust within yourself.

Practice 1: Gratitude

Each morning, list five new things to be grateful for—things you haven't named before. These can be small, simple, or profound.

Then, list three things you appreciate about yourself. It may be painfully uncomfortable at first, because you have become so accustomed to lying to yourself about your worth and harshly judging yourself. The truth may feel like the lie when you first begin this practice.

Stand in front of a mirror. Look into your eyes. Imagine the reflection is a dear friend who's been through everything with you. Tell her what you see. Thank her for her resilience. Compliment her strength. Speak love into her soul.

This is not false positivity—it's a recalibration of your relationship with yourself. Say only what you believe, and let that belief expand over time.

Practice 2: Self-Forgiveness

Self-forgiveness is the medicine for shame, guilt, and unworthiness. It unhooks you from stories that were never yours to carry.

Stand before the mirror. Picture your younger self—at any age. Speak directly to him/her. Offer the love and safety you needed then. Your parents and caregivers offered you what they knew how. Self-forgiveness allows you to be the parent, caregiver, and friend who can rewrite the stories of your past. Say aloud:

"I forgive you for..."

Or, "I forgive myself for..."

Forgive yourself for choices made in fear, for times you didn't know better, for beliefs you inherited. Forgive yourself for holding blame that was never yours.

Let the emotions come. This is healing work.

As you release old patterns, your life recalibrates. You begin to attract people and experiences that match your now-elevated self-worth. Some relationships may fall away. Let them. You have outgrown them. If they are also growing, they won't be far away.

Most importantly, you are not responsible for anyone else's happiness. You are not responsible for their perceptions. But you are responsible for how you show up for yourself. How you show up for yourself creates an example of what's possible for others, without the burden of carrying them on your shoulders into what you wish for them.

Make these practices part of your daily rhythm. As you do, your worth will no longer feel like something to chase. It will feel like home.

Reflection Questions:

- What is one thing I've never thanked myself for?

- What belief about myself am I ready to forgive?

- What would it look like to show up for myself daily?

_____

_____

_____

_____

_____

_____

Mirror Work Prompt

Stand before your reflection and say:

- "I see you. I honor you. I'm here for you now."

Then ask:

- What does this version of me need to hear?

- How can I show her (or him) more love today?

Let the answers rise from within. This is the practice. And practice makes peace. You are worth showing up for — every single day.

KEY #7
INTERNALIZE

THE 7TH KEY
Internalize Your True Worth

What does it mean to own your true worth?

Owning your true worth is more than a

mindset. It is a lived, fully embodied

knowing—one that becomes internalized so

deeply that no external force can shake it.

You were born whole, complete, and

perfect in alignment with who you are here

to be. Any judgment of your value is an

illusion of human conditioning. Worth is not earned. It is already given. It is remembered.

And like any form of remembering, it happens in layers.

Unshakable Internal Belief

Your entire life has been shaped by beliefs — some chosen, most inherited. The good news is that what was learned can be unlearned. What was borrowed can be returned. What was false can be released.

The process of internalizing your true worth begins by identifying the false narratives you've carried — and then replacing them with beliefs that reflect your truth.

The truth is in your core. It's the gut feeling, the inner voice, the quiet knowing that whispers, "You were never broken. You were born for greatness. You are divinity in motion." When your new beliefs align with this inner truth, they become powerful enough to transform your entire life.

Scientists refer to the gut-brain connection as a "second mind." This second mind is not ruled by logic or fear. It is your intuition – it is your connection to soul knowing. It is a higher truth speaking through you. When your beliefs match your intuition, you stop questioning your worth.

How Beliefs Become Biology

New beliefs take root through repetition, indoctrination, programming, and emotional resonance, until they become fully embodied.

Research shows that many of the cells in your body regenerate every 21 days. That means your biology is constantly updating. And you can program it with new instructions. When you hold a belief for 21 days, you don't just form a habit—you form a new identity. Your cells remember. Your energy changes. Your behavior shifts. And your results follow.

Hold those beliefs for another 21 days, and your former identity begins to feel like a distant memory. That is how powerful belief integration can be. This is how we rewire ourselves—not by force, but by frequency.

Internalization as Embodiment

To internalize is to embody. When a belief is fully embodied, it becomes automatic. It is Natural. Unquestioned. It becomes who you are.

- You no longer try to believe in your

worth. You simply know it.

- You no longer ask for permission to be seen. You are seen.

- You no longer hustle to prove your value. You own your value.

When this happens, everything shifts. Your work no longer defines you—it expresses you. Your income no longer validates you—it reflects you. You are no longer seeking worth in external achievements because you've reclaimed it from within.

And here's the magic: when your worth is internalized, the world mirrors it back.

You Are Not Your Work

As you integrate this truth, you begin to separate who you are from what you do. Your value is not your profession. It is not your productivity. It is not your pricing, your platform, or your popularity. Your value is intrinsic. Period.

The investment others make in your services may be shaped by the market, but your worth is not. One is external. The other is eternal.

You are who you are —invaluable,

powerful, influential, magnetic, unshakable
—no matter what you do.

Signs You've Internalized Worth

- You no longer tolerate relationships that dishonor your value.

- You confidently raise your rates or ask for what you deserve.

- You speak with clarity and no longer shrink to make others comfortable.

- You stop comparing yourself because you understand your uniqueness is your gift.

Most importantly, you feel peace. Not because everything is perfect. But because you no longer need perfection to feel worthy.

Final Thoughts

You are just as valuable as anyone who has ever lived—simply because you exist. Everything in the universe is designed to prosper and is coded for greatness. It's simply a matter of you remembering who you are. Let this truth become the new foundation of your life.

May your internalized worth radiate

outward into your work, your relationships, and your legacy.

You are not your old story. You are not your external metrics. You are not your doubt. You are the embodiment of remembered worth. You are love, you are divine expression, you are infinite creation, experiencing itself as you. With YOU, all things are possible.

And this is where your new story begins.

Reflection Questions:

• What belief have I fully released — and what has taken its place?

• How do I know I've internalized a new truth?

• What will I do differently now that I know my worth?

_____

_____

_____

_____

_____

_____

Integration Practice

For the next 21 days, choose one new belief that reflects your true worth. Write it down. Say it aloud. Feel it in your body.

Example: "I am worthy of abundance and prosperity, simply because I exist."

Repeat this every morning and every night. Let it become a part of you. Let it shape the way you walk, speak, create, and lead.

At the end of the 21 days, reflect:

- What shifted?

- How did life respond?

- What are you now ready to claim?

Cheers to your lifetime of personal and professional success—whatever that looks and feels like for you.

You've remembered who you are. And now, you live it.

_____

_____

_____

_____

_____

_____

CONCLUSION
You Were Always Worthy

Owning your worth isn't a final destination. It's a way of being — a daily return to your truth, your voice, and your intrinsic value.

If this book has done its job, you're no longer looking outside yourself for proof that you are enough. You know now: you always were.

You were born worthy. Whole.

Valuable beyond measure. That truth may have been forgotten, buried beneath other people's expectations, judgments, or projections — but it was never lost.

What you've done in these pages is remember. You've uncovered the beliefs that never belonged to you. You've questioned the stories that once felt permanent. You've dared to see yourself through new eyes — eyes of compassion, clarity, and power.

This is the beginning of embodied worth. As you move forward, remember:

- Confidence is not the starting point. It's the result of aligned action.

- Healing isn't about fixing yourself. It's about reclaiming yourself.

- Your voice is your authority.

- Your story is yours to shape.

Whether you're leading a business, raising a family, sharing your gifts, or simply learning how to love yourself in deeper ways — this inner work touches everything. The more you value yourself, the more value you bring to the world.

So keep practicing. Keep forgiving. Keep loving. Keep dreamweaving the story you came here to live. Keep writing the narrative and living the story you wish to tell.

Because when you own your worth — not someday, but now — you don't just change your life. You help to transform the world. You help change the narrative for everyone who comes after you. And that is no small thing.

You are worthy.

You are powerful.

And you are needed.

Welcome to your new story.

Welcome home to who you were born to be!

ABOUT THE AUTHOR

Victoria Reynolds is an intuitive futurist, media executive, and visionary architect of personal and planetary transformation. A former spiritual teacher turned executive leader, Victoria now serves as the Chief Operating Officer of Gnostic TV, where she is pioneering the next evolution of media, storytelling, and leadership.

Born into a high-control, polygamist

fundamentalist sect, Victoria spent the early part of her life unraveling deeply embedded stories of fear, shame, and unworthiness. Her personal journey — from escaping religious indoctrination and the fate of becoming a child bride to building conscious businesses and mentoring visionary creators — has become the foundation for her mission: to help others rewrite the narratives that limit their power and reclaim their inherent value.

A bestselling author of *Transcending Fear, Free Your Spirit,* and *Fearless and Free,* Victoria is known for her ability to bridge ancient wisdom with modern leadership. Her work blends soulful storytelling, spiritual insight, and strategic clarity to help individuals live, lead, and create from a place of wholeness.

Through books, talks, and media platforms, Victoria invites her audience to remember who they are, dismantle outdated belief systems, and become the authors of their own soul-scripted lives.

She believes that when you change your beliefs, you change your story — and when you change your story, you change everything. To explore her latest offerings or connect for speaking or consulting, visit:

VictoriaReynolds.com

www.ingramcontent.com/pod-product-compliance
Lightning Source LLC
Chambersburg PA
CBHW051840090426
42736CB00011B/1892